"Manual For Entrepreneurs".

If You Want To Be A Successful Entrepreneur, Surround Yourself With Eagles Because This World Is Full Of Flies.

AUTHOR: EDBERT JOSUE RIOS TORO.

"Think like an eagle and you will see the results ".

EDBERT JOSUE RIOS TORO.

If You Want To Be A Successful Entrepreneur, Surround Yourself With Eagles Because This World Is Full Of Flies.

Manual For Entrepreneurs.
February 2021.

Author-Editor:
© Edbert Josue Rios Toro.
Av. Universitaria Con Santa Rosa Paradero 2. Señor de Los
Milagros Block Q-Lot 62. San Martin de Porres.

Phone. +51 984 741 740.
influenciasmillonari as@gmail.com
Lima Peru.
First digital edition, January 2021.
E-book available: www.amazon.com
ISBN: 978-612-00-5872-5.

This book was created in order to promote "Self Help" through various life examples and reflective examples where I invite you to use your imagination so that you can understand the written illustrations.

The intention of creating this project is to express positive ideas that motivate young people to get ahead believing in themselves until they achieve their life purposes.

Do your best, and think big to achieve better results. Because fear does not go far.

This book is about the vocational guidance that all entrepreneurs must follow when fighting for our personal development and about how to seek motivation in ourselves, discovering what we are good for, since many times because of our innocence and lack of We end up asking for advice or listening to the words of the wrong people thinking that they will give us a great answer when expressing our ideas and for different reasons they end up cutting our wings so that we no longer continue dreaming, which creates mistrust in ourselves,That is why the development of this very important topic is a very strong concept for the ears of many, and at the same time it is very true for the motivation of other people who are not afraid to show the added value of their actions as entrepreneurs.

Think Like An Eagle And You Will See The Results.

Thanks.

Thank God, all powerful, beloved and heavenly father for allowing me to express myself through this project, which was shaped with the intention of helping other people, leaving them a previous review of my experiences to achieve my goals. And for allowing me to fulfill my life purpose which is to improve myself and move forward to show that dreams can be achieved as long as you are constant in your plans.

In the same way I want to thank my parents for the upbringing they gave me, my uncles, aunts, cousins and cousins for supporting me at all times.

To my friends for giving me that unconditional support and challenging me on opportunities for me to give my best, until I achieve good and better results in the activities that I performed as a worker, student, and apprentice among other tasks.

Many thanks to those people who helped me get to where I am, but without a doubt one of the best is you, my reader, reader who takes your valuable time to read this humble and outstanding work for your pleasure and moral support, thank you , many thanks.

Contents.

Foreword.

At the top of a mountain at the peak of karma and loneliness. Hiding is a very, very, very quiet, fast, insightful and intelligent bird with impressive eyes that can see at short and long distances and even when it is flying it can see for miles without losing track. This bird has a short and pointed yellow beak, its legs are the same color as its beak. Their wings can measure up to two (2) meters and a half (1/2). These are brown, white, and black. Their claws are so strong that they can take prey of up to 55 kilos and lift it to the sky without any problem. / This warrior and lord of the heights has a unique purpose which is to go out into the world and in search of his goal regardless of the weather or the conditions that are around him, demonstrating supremacy every time he goes out in search of success flying high as no other bird would have. Crowning himself as the king of the heights. Since for centuries it has earned the respect of its viewers. To the amazement of many, some call it the successful bird, entrepreneur of great feats and victories, while others visualize it with respect and majesty.

Now the most interesting thing about this bird is that it visualizes its target from a great predetermined distance of two miles which is equivalent to "3218.68 Meters" once while in the sky and without failing. At that distance we will call it "time". AND

It is a great road full of force with air currents that we still have to travel depending on the speed at which we undertake our projects. Determining the distance traveled, which will be the days, the hours, where our objective is in order to find the hunt for success.

Comparatives Of The Eagles With Human Beings:

Using imagination as a metaphor to achieve our dreams is part of creativity, the comparison of eagles and flies is a theme that can be developed by putting into practice only the creativity of the human being. To fully understand this topic I will give you a brief summary of the origin of eagles, their description, a series of similar comparisons and examples so that you can easily understand.

History: The eagle o Chrysaetos dates back more than 150 million years. This birdIt was synonymous with power for many ancient peoples because it was constituted as the symbol of majesty, power and victory throughout the centuries, that is why until today it is considered a symbol present in the iconography of various cultures such as Indu, Asian, European and Mesoamerican. It should be noted that it represented a large part of the Mochica / Moche culture of ancient Peru "Archaeological culture in the current province of Trujillo, was also represented in the culture of the Mayans and the Aztecs.

Description: It is said that an eagle can see, while it is flying, its target that is several kilometers away by following it stealthily from the heights to hunt it, it is one of the most preferred birds by a large majority of people is one of the birds with greater longevity, they are predators by nature, they are elegant hunters, very agile, fast and above all very silent, even going so far as to hunt their victim without realizing that they are in danger.

If she wants to, she can live to be 70 years old, but that depends on a big decision that she has to make when she reaches 40 years old. Already in his "fourth decade" he has to make a serious and difficult decision because at that age he has to go through a transformation phase to be able to renew his essence, that is, to obtain new feathers, a new beak and new claws.

*Discipline can be a fundamental ally for
Achieve your purposes, since intelligence represents the
ability or faculty to understand a specific topic,* but
discipline reflects the order of your thoughts and your
words, therefore you will know how much you are
prepared to act in the event of an eventuality or
entrepreneurship issue.

**It is better to be disciplined than to believe that you know
everything, otherwise the word undertake would not have
a joke, which means knowing how to identify the
opportunities that are presented to you by taking risks
investigating, ordering, thinking, acting.**

Rule Number 1.

Discipline Is Part Of Entrepreneurship & Success.

If you are not prepared to organize yourself & be more responsible with the commitments you have assigned, you will never achieve positive actions.

"A well-disciplined mind reflects the order & cleanliness around it, therefore through it the desire to get ahead is demonstrated, because we would be looking for the flaws, the imperfections that affect our image & life project."

Chapter 1.

The Representation Of The Eagle In The Life Of An Entrepreneur.

We adults are so distracted sometimes because when we grow up we forget to focus our attention directly on the children, we will have our reason to be absent, it is true, but it is still not an issue that you have to work tirelessly every day so that your family They do not lack anything because you are still missing you as direct support, ignoring that the first ally or entrepreneur may be your child. Brother (a), Cousin (a) Since they are the first people to realize what their purpose in life is and they are the first visionaries in the world because as they do not know about the evil that can surround them, they are interested in learning various themes through creativity, games, talks, and without forgetting that they reflect a great positivism with their tremendous as well as that they can make you laugh, cry or steal your heart, these friends like entrepreneurship for three reasons they are curious, they like to learn and they use their creativity to the fullest. For example.

Suppose on our way there are 3 tremendous "naughty" children they will be our cousins. 2 females and a male. The First Is Milagros, We will call her Lalito, she is a 10-year-old girl. Very beautiful and at the same time very tremendous, "surely if I had a twin sister they would connive a plan to tear down the house."

The second girl is 8 years old, her name is Charlotte, She is a very pretty girl, very innocent, playful and calm, she does not break a plate, "eye" when she is sleeping because otherwise she likes to chat, write, scratch things, run all over the house, eat sweets. But it is still a love of person like Milagros and José Gregorio, who by the way this 6-year-old boy is so tremendous that they almost call him to record the second part of Naughty Daniel as if it were a saga of the earthquake boy. But we still love our cousins, don't forget they are your cousins.

One day out of curiosity we are going to visit the children's mother, bone our aunt, "La Tía María". We are 26-year-old adults, hardworking, bitter, tired of everything, bored, in short we are toxic and negative. We arrive and greet the aunt, the cousins, and she invites us to come and eat and chat. "Pay close attention to this part that is interesting" they invited us to eat and while that happens our aunt. Games with children and says children greet their cousins and they greet you with those laughter and love that children reflect, but you are toxic and boring, that is, they reflect positivism and you are the negative that reflects bad habits. Saying within yourself that such annoying children won't let me eat. But you still greet them with that mischief. Meanwhile Our aunt Maria tells them. Children we are going to play in silence elsewhere, let your cousin eat in peace, let's go to the living room my loves. We are going to play that I am going to ask you things and you respond to see, to see

Mother: Charlotte, what do you want to be when you grow up, my precious baby, come on tell mom, tell me?

Charlotte: Teacher, teacher, teacher! Yesiiiiii.

Mother: To what good how much emotion my baby I will be a great teacher, I will help you to be a great teacher. My love!.

Mother: ¿Milagritos my beautiful girl, what do you want to be when you grow up, my girl??

Miracles: Doctor, to heal all my dolls and my patients! Yessss.

Mother: How well my girl will be a great doctor, you will be the best of all, my dear!

Mother: ¿And you my tremendous José. What are you going to do when you grow up?

Jose Gregorio: An old adult!

Mom: Hahahahaha No my dear, some activity that you like!

Jose Gregorio: Activity that I like, athlete Yes. Yes !.

While they were playing in the living room what they wanted to be when they grew up, you were eating a snack that your aunt prepared for you out of courtesy and because she loves you, and you were in the kitchen listening to everything they said and you just laughed at their words. Thinking that since they are children they don't even know what they want to be when they grow up and that, as well as how they behave they will be someone in life, you doubt it a lot, so it was better that it sounded like a joke.

Those who are already Aunt "Maria". I ask them what they wanted to do when they grow up and they innocently answered about their orientation or vision of the future because it is what they thought, suppose that the mother is proud and buys them the unexpected toys.

✓ For Milagros I buy her a notebook, pencils, a stethoscope, a white coat, surgical instruments "made of toys" and a large doll that serves as a practice for surgery.

✓ **Charlotte** I buy him a blackboard, some markers, crayons, white sheets and several dolls and small chairs pretending they are his students.

✓ **Jose Gregorio**: I buy him a soccer ball, several cones, sports clothes to practice, an archery, in order to awaken passion in sports and create a discipline.

Then time passes and we say goodbye to the cousins and the family because we had to undertake a trip to another country. "U.S". For work reasons and better quality of life. Once we go on a trip, we lose the reality of their lives and begin to live in another reality, another world.

Now imagine 16 years have passed. And the three kids grew up and liked it when they practiced every day to make it come true and fulfill their dreams.

➤ **miracles**There is now an enterprising woman, beautiful and intelligent, 26 years old, who since she was a child liked to play as a doctor, she decided to study medicine and thanks to the constant struggle, effort and perseverance of her and her parents she managed to graduate. Now she is a great medical surgeon specializing in oncology.

➤ **Charlotte**after scratching all the walls of the house, doing her homework, teaching her to add to her dolls, reading a story to them and learning to draw. She is a 24-year-old woman and she managed to study high school graduation at age 16, then she studied languages for 5 years, did a methodology and courses to specialize and is now a language teacher.

➤ **Jose Gregorio** He practiced soccer as if his life depended on it. He also studied high school, studied civil engineering until he also managed to graduate, but the most important thing is that he dedicated himself to sports and managed to enter the best soccer school in Venezuela. And he may be chosen as a striker to represent at the international Olympics that will be held in Qatar in 2022.

Without forgetting that you were in the "United States" and then one day you decide to return to Venezuela to see your family, and take advantage of the fact that it went well for you, you decide to invest in your country and procreate yourself by setting up some businesses because your cousins are already adults and they have changed a lot and fulfilled their dreams of becoming what they once dreamed of and you are totally amazed because you are not the only one who could progress and that they were learning every day and that they managed to undertake in their country.

Wow. Nobody really believes it. Hard to believe. All that is counted.

Now I ask?

What is more difficult to believe that these children during the 16 years that passed were entrepreneurs and were learning to take off from the nest, or that they were learning to fly with great expectations and that in the course of those 16 years that passed, they were able to see represented easily the sight of an eagle in the sky becoming the distance it would take them to hunt their prey and achieve success.

Surrounding ourselves with eagles is a very direct concept to the mindset of an entrepreneur, since if we compare ourselves with eagles we will better understand our life purpose and it will be easier for us to think about how to create a route to achieve success.

We are the average of the people we interact with, the music we listen to, the books, the newspapers we read, until we fill our brain with information and create habits or know a little more.

Everything happens for a simple reason that the body is programmed by the mind, and the mind is programmed by your essence, "your soul". And as such to achieve that balance you must study yourself to know what it is you want in life, since you must achieve that balance between body, mind and soul. In order to remove all the garbage that surrounds your brain, you must connect with the universe and cleanse your aura in order to shine with its own light. Only by focusing on the goal. You just have to think about it so from today I want you to prepare yourself to be the most successful entrepreneur and to develop a great work topic, and it is not a joke after reading this book ask yourself what you want for your future and if you are willing to achieve it.

Those people who surround themselves with influential entrepreneurs learn to fly faster than the rest of the entrepreneurs.

It is about growing in yourself by eliminating distractions to refresh your ideas so that you can use your mind like a parachute.

Rule Number 2.

"No Influence Is As Powerful As Positivism ".

If you are persevering and fight to achieve your dreams being constant day and night the inevitable will happen. Nobody will control your mind more than you, because you will learn to have your own criteria about what is good & bad for your future.

Negative people only serve to overshadow people who were born with their own lights, in some cases they serve to make them shine even more. Therefore, you have to use that darkness that they emanate as fuel and thus to get out of the mold. A simple example: "to be told that you cannot achieve something because they do not believe it is possible, you just relax, focus and in your mind say the following words with that positive force that will make you shine and exceed the limits of expectations: Ha Ha. Look how I do it.

Let yourself be carried away by millionaire influences, that is, successful people play the role of eagles. Negative people only represent flies, because they damage everything they touch with their bad energies. "

Episode 2.

The Eagle Motivation. / Believe In Ourselves By Having Discipline & Learning Not To Lower Your Guard In The Storm.

 The more persevering you are in life with your purpose, the closer you will be to achieving what you want, everything is in the habits that you put into practice, from your way of being, your way of thinking when executing a project, even the time to put your creativity into practice every day to be able to control your mind since only then can you control your future, otherwise you will be tied to your past and the backwardness that has kept you in your comfort zone or rather, that past dark that leads to poverty. Since your mind will be 75% programmed by the news, soap operas, the people you surround yourself with, the music you listen to and the education you receive.

 Do not feel bad about the changes, fatigue is part of the fight you are undertaking and the experiences are also part of the strength that you create in your character of personal motivation.

Being disciplined and believing in yourself plows you stronger every day, even if the road gets difficult and a thousand storms of negativity arrive, you just keep calm waiting for the right moment To take flight. Do not be afraid to fly or rather do not be afraid of what they will say remember that the sky is free and the wings are yours.

You decide whether to take flight in search of success or stay there at the bottom waiting for the storms to sweep away your dreams. You have to be constant to pursue success because it does not come by chance, you have to fight for it.

Many wonder how difficult it will be, and do not know that they have the answers themselves. "It all depends on the size of your ambitions and what you are willing to do to achieve it."

The road to success will be as difficult as you set your mind to and how high you decide to fly.

How So, Edbert?

You ask me, and I can tell you that the path to glory has never been so easy, not even for those who had fame. So they had to believe in himself even when things got difficult and no one helped them, even when their minds wanted to keep fighting and their bodies reneged on exhaustion and doubted what was happening yet they did not give up, they continued Standing up in battle, they kept fighting to achieve their goals and they persevered with what they wanted and did not rest until they saw their dreams materialized.

And the best part you know what it is?

That the feeling of winning with nothing compares because you and only you. You will know how much it cost you to get to the position you want to achieve. From that moment you will be a winner and your baptism of fire will begin, you will be an eagle, in search of success, in search of new challenges, new challenges, reviving your pride and your passion for what you want to do. That will be the reward for so much sacrifice and so much struggle. Which is why you decided not to listen to anyone else but yourself.

If you want to learn to fly like non-living eagles surrounded by flies, take your flight as high as possible!

Get advice from people who really leave you a good education and if someone comes to criticize you, do not let it affect you, or stop you with its bad vibes, it is time to go hunting for success.

Rule Number 3.

Being an entrepreneur is something that can only be explained in four broad and abstract words. "Believe In Yourself" Which is the same as creating your own visions of the future. Because only then can you open your mind to take on new challenges and seek a solution in general that benefits many people.

In life there is no such specific manual to achieve success so easy, since no one is going to tell you that it will be a matter of hours or a week for you to achieve it, take this into account if you really want to achieve your dreams. The only easy things you can accomplish in this life are:

Live off the hurt of others so that others feel sorry for your misery or live on excuses to cover up your own mistakes and continue as if nothing had happened.

Those two actions will lead you directly to failure because they will turn you into a mediocre person.

Chapter 3.

The Influences Of Flies. Destroy or damage everything in its path with the aim of feeding on human misery or the triumphs of others.

In general, these types of people maintain a negative energy field around them since they have not matured emotionally, they only reflect insecurity and selfishness to those they contact, since they think that if they do not do well, others will not do very well. well despite the frustrations they have in their little fly brain.

How to identify them?

Many of these people like to enter into conversations with the exchange of ideas turning them negative and absorbing that allows them to discharge their frustrations.

Thus, they turn their victim into one of the many through a simple negativity therapy invading their limits and decentralizing them, focusing on looking only at the defects and the negative part of things to compensate for their deficiencies and insecurities in order to feel better about themselves. without adding something positive to the conversation.

That is why toxic people often end up upsetting their victim, who ends up experiencing negative emotions feeling that their energy and joy are consumed.

A Simple Example Is: When after establishing a conversation with a negative person who does not care about life or who has no aspirations to get ahead, he sees that you are about to change your future through your thoughts and actions, he arrives and you He says that you are crazy or that they already did it and it did not work, why do you try if you are not going to achieve it because he or she does not believe you are capable of achieving it and you are convinced of what you are doing and the character that You are creating through the undertaking of your project, even if that person insists, and insists, and insists and continues insisting with the same thing, it is obvious that he does not want to help you and does not want you to improve yourself but

See how to end all stressed because of a frustrated person who in his miserable life did not learn to get ahead, to fly high.

It is not your fault that that person has not learned to take off from the nest and does not know how to fly high and settle for misery, trying to damage everything he touches with his negative influences.

Why the hell do you have to listen to them?

If the good or the damage is for you, success is for you and the experiences will be for you, that is where we have to learn to have our own criteria and send them to fry monkeys or to see if they already put the pig, "as they would say in my town" And it's not a joke, I'll tell you, I'll tell you and I'll repeat it to you again if that person is of no use to you, the hell they have to go. You simply have to add and not subtract, although they may be uncomfortable, the more valuable is your future and your well-being.

Success is yours so go for it do not let anyone cut your wings, remember that the sky is free and you decide if you want to fly or stay there, letting negative people with fly brains affect your well-being and they only fly low and live on misery.

When those envious people tell you that you are crazy because you are undertaking a new project or developing habits or doing what you like, and people come to tell you that you are crazy or that you are surely missing a screw, just calm down, breathe fresh air , smile and sarcastically and tell them.

Are you sure I'm crazy and that I am missing a screw, haha a screw ... just one?

I have about 10 screws missing, so I am a great entrepreneur and I will be a better person every day. Those screws that I am missing are the ones I did not need so I throw them away on the way.

Those screws were called.

- ✓ Stress.
- ✓ Fatigue.
- ✓ Apathy.
- ✓ Weakness.
- ✓ Be Negative.
- ✓ Conformity.
- ✓ Mental Poverty.
- ✓ Irresponsibility.
- ✓ Envy your neighbor.
- ✓ You want to gossip.

Those are the screws that I am missing so I am determined to fight to make my dreams come true.

To be an eagle entrepreneur, you must bear in mind that training and intelligence are important, although attitude and personality are what give character to your entrepreneurial character, that's where that desire to improve yourself comes. yourself and go after the hunt for success because he is not going to come to you you have to be persistent and go for him at all costs.

Go! ¿What are you waiting for?

How can we identify this type of person with the personality of a fly, that is, with negative influences.
They generally meet the following characteristics.

They think that life owes them something and that if they don't get what they want in 3 days it's not for them so it's not worth trying to keep trying.

They complain about everything if they do nothing in return to improve things.

They are frustrated people who believe that because they did badly on a profession issue, you will also do badly.

They criticize and criticize you until you feel insecure about what you are doing and surely when you achieve it they are the first people who are there to say that they supported and believed in you when in fact they have criticized you all along.

Like flies try to steal your plate of food they try to steal your triumph, or damage what they touch with their bad energies

Comparative of the Eagles and the Flies.

An Entrepreneur Eagle.

Is a
And Formidable
With a purpose
Because you always have one
Own & Besides That
To Move On & By
Your Goals Trying
Likewise Day by Day.

Agile.
Warrior.
Unique.
Initiative.
Struggle.
Attain
Surpass yourself.

That is the fundamental basis of an entrepreneur, eagle being a unique warrior, who was born to show the world what he is made of and what his life purpose is, because he believes in himself.

People With
　　　Syndrome
　　　　　Of The Flies.

Persons	*Miserable.*
That they always want	*Opacar.*
To a dreamer,	*Underestimating*
The desire you have	*Grow*
Like a true entrepreneur	*Eagle.*
Looking for the negative side of	*Always.*
everything	
& They won't let you grow professionally.	

Here the joke is told alone, this is how people with the fly syndrome act, they do not want you to overcome yourself because they love negativism and live from human misery, for something they underestimate you and it is not precisely to push you to get ahead They don't want you to improve yourself because they are afraid of being displaced.

You just get inspired by this image and remember that person who underestimated you and told you several times that you would not achieve your life purpose, because that project does not work and you are not prepared for it, Yo que tú, I breathe deeply and in my mind I meditate And I say, Ha, Ha, look how I do it.

Mathematics is influential in the life of an entrepreneur to calculate ideas and the speed at which we will execute our plans.

Knowing this we must write down all the ideas we have to carry out a project in a notebook with the help of a pencil. That would be the main thing to start with.

Rule Number 4.

All entrepreneurship begins with a small idea, some topic or someone that motivates us to achieve it by discovering that purpose.

That would be a good base to start if we propose we have to be more risky to make it happen, this is something as simple and as complicated as mathematics. Why?

Because of all the rules that I am mentioning, never forget this one, since it is one of the most important. "in life all our projects and actions are like mathematics. Positive results are only reflected according to how we develop our operations or strategies to obtain a positive result.

If there is an exponential "E", which in this case will be us in the face of so many mathematical changes over the years, from the negative influences that surround us, we must maintain that self-esteem and positivism being the exponential or rather the maximum expose "e" of overcoming. Because people who have managed to get ahead have done it through the "constant" constant struggle to overcome day and night and they did not give up, so do not give up and be the exponential that follows the constant. Through the "derivative" of your actions.

Because everything you do in the present will affect or benefit your future. Given this, you only have one thing left, "extract the common factor" so that it does not affect you and your life is better in terms of entrepreneurship. Here the common factor is any negative person who wants to affect your future, remember that you are the maximum exponential "e", no matter how much they try to change you, they will never achieve it because your value is 1 (one) only. Their is less than yours because it varies, so they will never be the same as you.

Chapter 4.

Undertaking From Scratch, How To Do It & What Are The Necessary Tools To Undertake.

To give you a clear idea of how to start from scratch I will briefly tell you a review of the crisis in my country and my personal experience on how I emigrated with my sister and friends to Peru in search of a better quality of life in a new path starting from zero despite the political, social and economic crisis that my country has been going through for more than 7 years to the present.

My testimony:I am a young entrepreneur just like you. 27 years old, born in Venezuela, a country where I grew up until I was 24 years old and I had to emigrate in October 2017. Despite the great political, economic and social crisis that my country is currently experiencing because of a political model that has been promoted by idiots. Sorry, sorry for some idiots, and a thief who calls himself "President of the Republic of Venezuela" and his string of useless people who do nothing but steal and deceive people. I say, I say "Administrative Cabinet", that all they have done is try to dissolve some business models just for the fact of wanting to have control of imports, Foreign Exchange, Resources, Private Sector Companies violating government agreements and treaties

Confusing the steps that correspond to a president and his work team with the obligations of the State. Through the misnamed Socialist Revolution, which has only brought misery, devaluation of the local currency "El Bolívar", Poverty and more poverty. This happened only because of wanting to suffocate the business model, killing its allies, running out of resources, it should be noted that Venezuela is among the 10 (Ten) richest countries in oil.

Since 1999. Until 2013. That its founder HRCF died. After that, for a period of transition, he assumed the position of El Burro. At that time, we were all happy, there was no problem until the crisis erupted and there are many people who did not expect this to happen, that is, to see how a country, which is a power producer of oil with one of the largest reserves in the world, Gold producer, Coltan, Diamante, with the fourth largest water dam in the world among others.

Personally, Venezuela had nothing to envy other countries regarding its landscapes, tropical climate, beaches, traditions, culture, it was a privilege, almost a wonder to live there, because it was like a woman in development, that each day it became more and more beautiful, and it was growing, and as it was to be supposed so much beauty is in danger in the wrong hands since the rulers of our country led us to the worst economic crisis that had ever seen in history to the point that they avian people who could not get medicine, food, much of the basic services disappeared, total madness.

In that year 2013. When everything collapsed I was studying civil engineering and working in a radio station, of course the crisis began to affect everything equally, displacing social classes (rich, business sector, middle class people, working class, independent workers , poor people, and so on) from there I touched the difficult choice of emigrating to other countries, that was a boom, because more than 8 million Venezuelans emigrated to different nations leaving everything that it cost us to obtain, taking all our dreams in a suitcase of 23 kilos, at that time we had to start from scratch, because we did not have a roof to reach, many of us were professionals already with careers in our country and we had to look for informal jobs or work on the streets to be able to survive and help our families economically from the outside.

Many people decided to emigrate to other countries either by land or by plane, 70% of the immigrants did so by land near the sister republic of Colombia, which was one of the nations that supported us by taking the step to move forward, in my In this case, my family and I were worried about the passing of our days, our future because we went through great calamities knowing that the country where you grew up was going through a strong economic crisis that seemed to have no way out.

One day I was working on the radio when suddenly one Sunday one of my sisters called me to tell me about her plans to emigrate to another country, but that she was still studying what country it would be and I with all the pride and happiness that I gave when I heard those words of entrepreneurship and motivation, I said, go ahead sister because no, I support you 100%, you are young, and you have the right to make your life, you also have a great future ahead of you, without any reproach I said these words to me. I support you, I congratulate you for thinking like this.

After 2 weeks it was when we met in person and she told me about her entrepreneurial plans and emigrating to Peru with her husband Franklin, 1 month later that is how they left in search of new adventures and desires to improve themselves, already being a 21-year-old woman at the time and my brother-in-law Francklin a visionary 25-year-old man also wanting to get ahead.

By the date of July they emigrated, I still had some career plans, I still remained in my comfort zone, I also had to make a decision because the crisis limited me to grow as a person because it was affecting me by work, study, and want better things and a better future with my family, who always supported me in all matters of entrepreneurship and personal development.

Although I liked my work on the radio, in construction and my career, at the end of 2017. I had to emigrate to Peru on a bus, traveling through 4 countries in 6 days which were extraordinary experiences, the change that was reflected in my something Incredible since it was a total success to travel 4 nations with total pleasure and the greatest affection towards Venezuelans, when arriving in Lima, Capital of Peru. There is this sister with my brother-in-law, it was not easy for me to adapt to so many changes, because, although they were there waiting for me they were a couple and needed privacy, so I had to find a rental and live alone, look for another job and start from scratch. What I liked the most was that he learns new tactics, strategies I decided to leave my room and look for work in the capital was when at that time I met my boss, a man over 40 years old owner of 6 restaurants, wise man with great character and an expert in business, like me since The boy had aspirations to get ahead, raise his family, create businesses, and grow emotionally and spiritually. He gave me a job as a waiter in one of his restaurants in his own way, his workers taught them many things saying eloquent phrases and said one phrase among so many that until the sun today remained engraved in my mind

"<< Even To Save Money You Have To Grow Up >>
"Wow. It is easy to pronounce and very strong at the same time. The man was absolutely right. As we want to achieve glory if we do not propose it, we must mature, we just have to read a little more, thank God for a new day, be persistent in our objectives to achieve our goals.

By that time the year was approaching and I was living alone in my room, and while I was working in the restaurant and carrying out my work I was thinking of something bigger, in a better position in a better economic position, so I needed to create several memorable projects to achieve greater economic income towards my pocket, it was at that time when I thought about many things and above all that I did not have a good financial education, that I did not know how to save money, how to create assets even when I slept, and I was confused because Who was going to ask him for advice if he had no friends or family who studied economics, I remembered my boss Mr. Francisco and it was then that I went to an internet booth and looked for information in the major economics books as they are Google, and YouTube,Since there was the real virtual screen where the largest record of information was found and after watching documentaries and projects on entrepreneurship it occurred to me to make a book are the life of eagles through entrepreneurship since they have a certain resemblance to us beings human besides that they represent the sign of majesty, victory and strength.

One of the greatest influences that filled me with positive ideas was documenting myself about the great titans that drove the world as they were:

- **John David Rockefeller:** He was an American businessman, investor and industrialist, who worked in the oil industry, reaching the point of monopolizing it in 1870, founded with his collaborators the "Standard Oil Company", the largest oil company in the United States.

- **Andrew Carnegie:** The intern and activist who bought the << competitor Homestead Steel Works >> company, which had a huge plant together with the supply of coal and iron mines, a long railway line 1892 only created the company << Carnegie Steel Company >>. The empire of steel.

- **Cornelius Vanderbilt:** The king of the railroad industry that communicated and carried heavy loads in much of the United States in the year 1860. If Company was called Vanderbilt it was the Accessory Transit Company Ferry Empire.

➢ **John Pierpont Morgan:** He was an American businessman, banker, and art collector who dominated the corporate finance and industrial consolidation of his day. Its activities include JP Morgan. He contracted Thomas Alva Edison to present him with an innovative project that would revolutionize the time and TA Edison, I present the project of the direct current DC << Edison General Electric and Thompson-Houston Electric >> Company to form the "General Electric Company "In 1892.

➢ **Nicola Tesla**: He was the creator of the AC Alternating Current in the 1880s. He was a brilliant scientific genius, former assistant scientist Thomas Alva Edison, / Tesla was an eccentric whose inventions allowed mass communication systems to achieve power. Tesla had an eidetic memory, which meant that he could recall images and objects very accurately. This allowed him to accurately visualize 3D objects, and as a result, he was able to build working prototypes using few preliminary drawings.

➤ **Henry Ford**: The founder of the business company <<
Ford Motor Company >> and father of the modern
production lines used for the mass production of
automobiles in 1903. He promoted the manufacture of a
large number of low-cost automobiles through the
production chain.

Among other great titans of large industries that will be
remembered throughout history for their great feats to
achieve success and promote the world of technology. I
invite you to watch the documentary Giants of the big
industries on YouTube. It will be a great start to change
your mind. I guarantee it, there are 8 chapters and it lasts
about 30 minutes each.

Dare to fly like eagles because fear does not go far.
Success can be hunted from the heights, otherwise you
will learn to fly like flies.

Rule Number 5.

Studying a project for a certain time and then risking to execute it is part of growth, if you fall you can get up as many times as necessary to find the successful hunt. But if you don't try, you will be left with the desire to know if in the future you could see it succeed or not. So leave the fear that not everything has to be so perfect to achieve something, it is just a matter of risking more and leaving the fear well stored in the drawer.

Learning to take off from the nest means putting fear aside by challenging yourself to do new things without fear of what they will say. Get out of the comfort zone. "Get inside the character, believe in yourself. Only then will you learn to fly like eagles."

Chapter 5.

Learning To Take Off From The Nest.

The eagles' learning process consists of taking off from the nest learning to fly 3 months after their birth, these birds seek to take flight leaving their comfort zone preparing to face new challenges which is another great test to gain experience and resistance, that is the message of entrepreneurship in analyzing ourselves to learn new things and say conformism aside, for this we must find a way to take off, you have to take something into account the only security that ensures your success is the security of believing in yourself and in no one else, without hypocrisy, it is just as it sounds, first think of yourself, believe in yourself, live for yourself, fight for yourself, because only for you is success.Only you who knew the process of fighting towards victory will know how much effort and sacrifice were worth.

Eagles are wise, by nature they have a great future development mindset. Although it sounds offensive, literally the saying of "surround yourself with eagles because this world is full of flies, is a basic and simple concept that can be interpreted in many ways, such as entrepreneurs are often young eagles that We are in our comfort zone that can be represented as a nest and that is why we have to learn to discover our direction, our horizons,

In this process is when our mentors who are our parents teach us to fly to fend for themselves, from the moment we are born, we learn to speak, to eat, to go to school. Up to 16 years old. In many cases.

It's time to fly high, to dream big, to look in the mirror and yell at yourself, I'm not going to give up so easily, I'm not going to give up so easily, I can with this, I can with all tests necessary to get ahead, because this is a battle of resistance and mental struggle the other 20% is emotional, so it is time to show what you are made of, to show what your purposes are, your ambitions, today is the big day to prove.

Because today is the great day to get out of the nest, "get out of that comfort zone" which keeps us spiritually inactive and takes away our desire to live and motivate ourselves.

It is time to believe in ourselves, it is time to seek to reach our limits, it is time to grow spiritually and emotionally to achieve our goals and move forward, because if we do not believe in ourselves we will not fulfill our life purposes. And it is enough to remember that time is running out, if we go through the cemetery, we will see a cruel and harsh reality, that above the grave there is a tombstone that describes the name of the person and (2) two very important dates that They are the day of birth and the day that said person died, those (2) two dates represent an important message which says that life is one,

When the reality is that our actions change the world contributing our grain of sand by the fact of becoming beings of motivation through our faith and infinite will to make something happen in this world so precious and so beautiful that God has given us .

Let us remember that time is running out for us to be wasting our time next to those who are not worth it, next to unnecessary activities that do not contribute anything to the development of humanity or our own development. Our time started running out from the day we were born. So let's not waste it fooling around with the wrong people.

One of the biggest influences for your personal growth can be your family or even your partner. They can be one of your best allies. In such a big entrepreneurship project & as simple as the life project.

A simple example is living in pairs: if you must support each other until you form an alliance of mutual affection, think about each other, until you form a single thought and then take the next step of granting the miracle of life, that miracle will be the smallest moment of happiness that reflects all that feeling and positivism for which they decided to undertake as couples thinking of only one until they want to achieve it and realize that your greatest entrepreneurial project is the family. And as a living example of what we are saying, it will be to see what is reflected in your children. In your roots, That is one of the most valuable endeavors to see the positive side of life.

In the last case, your partner does not turn out to be what you expected. Because if we analyze something about boyfriends, everything is beautiful. For the simple reason that dating is the art of cheating on the other person because we can come to think that everything will be perfect because no one swears, no one blows a gas, no one burps, no one speaks ill of anyone, because it only matters the happiness that both of them reflect at that moment. And then time passes they decide to live with that person or try something and you discover that your Romeo, or Your Juliet was not what you expected because they have already entered into trust and decided to show their true personalities. Bone "Take Out The Claws".

At first everything was beautiful, it was happiness and harmony, but then as time goes by you realize that you are one of the people who likes to play sports, study, read, learn many things and you like order and cleanliness because that's how they disciplined you at home and, but nothing to that person that you point out because they see it boring. And you try to change your habits for that person. That's where negativity influences you.

"Eye is not a matter of machismo, it is a matter of personal attitude" that is, of the person who reflects it, it does not matter in sex, what matters is how he acts, whether man or woman. Let's remember rule number 3. That talked about discipline because it is part of entrepreneurship and success.

If we weren't Ready and Organize us to be more responsible with our commitments, we were never going to achieve positive actions. This example in pairs applies to the current rule and the previous ones.

In the same way, do not feel bad about it if your partner does not know about your plans little by little you can tell them or give them this book in physical form so that they understand a little more about visionary ideas, remember that men make women and women makes the man.

That's when we learn to take off from the nest by growing in ourselves, leaving fear behind, putting the desire to learn every day and at the same time putting into practice those teachings that we obtain along the way.

An Entrepreneur Does Not Need Limits To Meet His Goals.

Rule Number 6.

If you want to fulfill your dreams, focus on having a fixed base so that you can hunt your prey. Eagles are very intelligent, fast and raptor birds that study the conditions of the environment that surrounds them for miles or around them in order to know what is the battlefield they are facing to hunt their prey. In addition to the fact that when they enter a battlefield they are the most feared birds due to the incredible influence they wield.

Chapter 6.

Eagles Always Fly High.

These birds only go down to land if it is necessary on many occasions to hunt their prey, so do not let your guard down even to breathe, remember that you can go as far as your dreams allow you.

From there we will know the added value of the and the motivation effort makes the personality. How the character of success is created with his own effort.

Those who do not think big will not see their dreams grow, much less will be able to fly through them, remember that if we put our minds to it we can go as far as our dreams allow us.

Don't give up, come on, what are you waiting for, go ahead, go ahead, you still haven't given your best. Your dreams are worth a thousand other people's thoughts. Remember that each head is a world & that world can only coexist if the mind is used properly to give oxygen to the thoughts.

Those who judge you today. They are just a bunch of mediocre judges who believe themselves to determine your luck and be able to demand your will because they believe better than you and they think that you will not be able to achieve it.

Although Plato said it when he was inspired by the legendary phrase that said "EAGLE DOES NOT HUNT FLY" It is the most illustrated way to reflect that people with great responsibilities should not engage in small activities that are the responsibility of other people.

The Eagles are forced to perform great feats to find the hunt for success without wasting time.

Rule Number 7.

Focus on your goals regardless of the criticism or adversity that surrounds you. For this you have to be like the eagles, you just need to focus on your goal, eliminating distractions completely.

It all depends on the magnitude of your project so to learn how to hunt your prey. Study that project that you want and like so much during an established learning process. Just as eagles at 40 years of age do a renewal process for 3 months to fly again, so we have to do, although this can be short to long term. Remember that practice makes perfect.

Chapter 7.

Learn To Hunt Your Prey.

Educate yourself, inform yourself, practice, trust yourself, be optimistic and persistent. This world is made to develop and grow, not to wait for a miracle to happen, if you fail 10 times try 20 more times until you achieve perfection or be close to it.

¡Whoever gets close to a good tree, gathers good fruit!

Have you ever heard the saying, Eagle Doesn't catch Flies, this is a saying which is inspired by Plato. Who was a great philosopher, the saying comes from Latin. (Aquila non capit muscas). Which translates a very strong meaning exemplifying that eagles are very powerful, fast and intelligent birds. They are only dedicated to hunting large prey and achieving great goals.

Eagles always fly high, they only go down to the ground to hunt their prey or for a very strong objective so that this is their will to descend from the skies, they are very rapacious and very intelligent birds. The best of all is that they go out to conquer the world from the heights, and when they go out into nature. They scare smaller animals, because they know that if they don't react they become the prey.

If you want to achieve something just go for it. Fight for it if you fall a thousand times it shows that you can get up ten thousand times.

How can I do it?:

➤ **Set short-term and long-term goals.**

The main thing would be to take a pencil and a paper so that you can start writing your daily, weekly, monthly and even annual goals. Since without any goal that we propose in life and without any effort to make our dreams come true, we will be lost.

➤ **Establish good habits daily.**

These habits are the building blocks of success. Successful people have many good habits and few bad ones. And what habits do we consider good?

These include watching television little, reading a lot, continuously training, for example. In short, these habits are the best way to learn from others and avoid mistakes that we could make.

➤ **do exercise.**

Practicing exercise will make you a more energetic and at the same time more productive person. In addition, with sport you will not only get a better physique and greater self-esteem, but you will also face more challenging situations that you did not do before out of fear.

> **Feed your soul, mind and body.**

When I say that you have to feed the body, I mean that you have to give it pleasure, security, keep it energetic and safe if necessary in order to achieve greater positive responses.

As far as feeding the mind and soul, it is nothing more than surrounding ourselves with people who lead to positive influences, as I like to call them. <PEOPLE WITH MILLIONAIR INFLUENCES> because those people will give us a million ideas to be successful. Keep in mind that great friendships can help you reach your goals faster; Also, we must do what we really like and dedicate our time to things that make us truly happy.

> **Every now and then we have to give ourselves a well-deserved rest.**

People who believe that resting is not being productive are less productive because you have to know how to stop when your mind is exhausted. Ideally, strike a balance between work and rest to increase your productivity. Otherwise, our performance in the activities that we undertake will decrease, since the mind controls the body and the body itself and itself is manifested through ideas.

> **Plan and prioritize.**

Do not leave for tomorrow what you can do today. Make a list of things you have to do and do the most important ones, do not go to the next activity without having finished the previous one, pursue your goal until you achieve it, whatever the cost. And set time limits for completing the task.

> **Manage money.**

Once working in a restaurant, I heard my boss say in a work meeting that even to mature, you have to learn to save money. That was a very simple phrase but until the sun today it impacted my mind because it gave me to understand that when you start a business or a project you can measure your degree of vocational maturity through decision making knowing what it is. you really need to achieve it, and one of those purposes is to know how to manage your ideas to use resources since money is a necessary tool to fulfill your dreams.

So the basic solution is to change our consumer mentality to a mentality with a view to investing in the future. Because spending money wisely will make you grow as a person and include your business.

➤ **Know your strengths.**

We all have strengths and weaknesses, or flaws and virtues. To achieve success it is essential to enhance those strengths that we all have, and that we sometimes hide, to improve and not have so many weaknesses that limit us to fulfill our life purpose.

➤ **Improve your capabilities.**

Focus on how you can improve yourself and be better than you already are. To achieve this, focus on getting the formula to be the best person in the next 30 days, do not forget to grab a pencil and a notebook to write down your ideas if you will have a clear vision of what you want for your future.

You do not believe me, imagine that you take a pencil and that that will be the time you have to write what will happen in the book of your life and that each time it is ending that will be the time that you will be running out, the difference here is that you decide how to spend your time and your life.

Let's do another reflection exercise and think for a moment that your life is a box of blank sheets and that each day that begins is a blank sheet in which we decide how to fill in that sheet, whether to place it an exciting title, whether to write our future or let others come and write what happened in our lives. Now what I'm saying makes sense or doesn't make sense. Every day that passes is a lived page and as the years go by you will know which was the most exciting chapter in your life, or you will know how much your time was worth in your life project.

➢ **Visualize yourself. << Learn to Know Yourself >>.**

Improve the image you have of yourself and the world around you so that your goals grow towards higher goals. People tend to have pessimistic thoughts like "I'm not good enough at this" or "I'm not capable of this." These thoughts limit and discourage us, but frankly what limit you are not these perceptions, in fact, it can be changed for the better, but what limits you is the way you perceive yourself and those around you. A good exercise to visualize myself as I want is to write it and visualize the way I will act in the most difficult moments. By repeating this process, little by little those thoughts will become reality.

Poverty is in the mind, not the wallet, not in a bank account.

Therefore, if you want to be successful, study the environment in which you find yourself a lot and, above all, study the people with whom you surround yourself very well. Since many of them suffer from CRONOS syndrome.

Rule Number 8.

Surrounding yourself with negative people does not add anything to your future plans. In this case, if the phrase applies, tell me who you are with so I can tell you who you are. Eagle or Fly?

Negativism is not part of entrepreneurship with that you are only going to make your brain "shrink", that is, you will be amazed by ideas. Since negative people live on gossip, problems, disorder, bad life & most importantly they damage everything they touch.

Chapter 8.

How Does Surrounding Yourself With Misery Affect Your Future?

Dream stealers are those people who judge you, criticize you, envy you, speak ill of you and never offer you something good to grow as a person since they only like to intimidate and threaten. But you remember that ignorance has no limits and this <NEGATIVE INFLUENCE> is an ally of dream stealers.

If you really want to succeed, do not stop and work on that project that you dream of so much, let's go wait, you know how you can achieve it, work in silence, do not tell anyone about your plans, unless it is yourself looking at yourself in it. mirror and reflecting your own ideas in a pencil and notebook. If you tell people about your plans that if they know about limits and live in the comfort zone, you will only be able to stop yourself because they will tell you that it will not work and that you better dedicate yourself to looking for a job. That it is better to grow up and not think about stupid things, when not even they know the stupid things they are saying because they limit themselves and live like slaves forced to follow the same routines every day.

Getting out of bed, washing up, going to work, letting others decide what to do with their time for 12 hours a day almost every day, then coming home to get ready to eat, wash again, and sleep. And that's how life goes, if that can be called life being a slave to the system, all that just to get a minimum amount of money and be able to cover their basic expenses until it is over and then return to the same routine.

If you already know this, ask yourself looking in the mirror, what are you waiting for? It is time to show all those people who did not believe in you that you can do more than they imagine, because they underestimate you but they are not able to see more. Beyond reality, and that reality is that you are feeding on all that negativity to get ahead, since that negativity is part of the fuel you needed to get ahead, that you only needed a motivation, someone who would challenge you to be able to go further than you think.

Since if we start to believe the words of other people who only see us with destructive criticisms or judge us by our appearances without even knowing us, there would be the real problem. Which would be the lack of decision making and own criteria. To get things done. Ask yourself something you are going to pay attention to a person who lives their life criticizing others, if you want you can take it to heart and make it people and annoy you to the point that you feel dissected from the vocation you want to carry out. Take a look at his profile and you will realize if his life is more miserable than your life. It is a starry phrase, but it is the truth because you pay attention to a person who is below your personal aspirations and who lives complaining all the time.

I don't see the joke. It doesn't make me laugh, personally I take a good look at who that person is and if they don't represent anything to me, I send them to shut their mouths immediately, to show them that they have no power over me and that their opinions are worth nothing at that moment .

Since their life is more miserable and they spend it criticizing other people who really want to get ahead, that is, perhaps the old gossip or the negative gift Mr. are part of your achievements, your air, your day to day . As for you to pay attention to them.

They are not the ones to come cut your wings and decide your luck. The fact that they have not dared to become entrepreneurs does not mean that you cannot achieve your goals.

My mother as a child told me, with people like that around you, they only manage to delay the future of a country. And it sounds like a joke, but it is something metaphorical and real, my mother said it because she was a businesswoman, she and my family had greengrocers and they harvested the fruits of the land. Anyway; The reflection resembles that people like this only look for a way to deconcentrate you because they do not have a clear objective to fulfill their life purpose and they deconcentrate those who want to seek their life purpose or ask yourself the following questions.

Perhaps Thomas Alva Edison would have been encouraged to create more than a thousand inventions that would revolutionize the world, among them the electric light bulb, carbon microphone, nickel iron batteries, electric vehicle, kinetoscope, phonograph stand out. Mimeograph, Dictaphone, Electricity distribution system, among others only using the theory of DC Direct Current. Among others.

John David Rockefeller: He would have been encouraged to create Standard Oil. As the largest oil industry in the US handling 95% of the crude. Until discovering the potential it had.

Andrew Carnegie: It would have powered the steel industry, or it would have created Carnegie Hall. Among other great geniuses, you just keep that calm and surround yourself with positive people who help you grow or hang out with people who only make fun of everything that happens in life for any stupidity, remember that the human study has no limits.

Negative influences do not allow you to develop as an entrepreneur. They are only looking for the necessary strategies to clip your wings.

Make mistakes as many times as necessary to achieve your goal if you fall 10 times, go for your success, try 20 more times if necessary, but see for it that fear does not go far.

Rule Number 9.

 Surrounding yourself with toxic and negative people does not help your future at all, with this you will only attract bad influences into your life until you become one of the many. If you are one of those who believe that studying a lot in life will do you good, sooner or later you will fail along with that theory. So remember this. You are not what you study you are what you reflect as a person if you are problematic you will only attract problems. If you are joy, joy you are going to attract into your life. Everything is relative until it is contagious in the people around you.

 Now imagine being present in a place where you have to share with negative people, whether they are thieves, drug addicts, gossipers. Corrupt. For a year. What do you think you are going to learn? If the brain is a sponge that absorbs and processes the information that we send to it through our thoughts, that's why they are the comparisons between an eagle & a fly. They are the same comparisons of a tireless warrior who struggles to fulfill his dreams & a negative person who complains about everything in life & they see everything as a game until they give bad examples.

Chapter 9.

Learning From My Mistakes.
Taking flight so as not to be just another fly.

In the course of my training as an entrepreneur, I learned to be curious and to fight for my dreams at any cost, so much so that I did not give up on the road, although it became more and more difficult and that was the most exciting thing, than when you are a A person focused on what you want to achieve, you are willing to learn even if this implies learning from your mistakes, the lesson that this topic leaves is that entrepreneurs are people with a great curiosity to learn things, even if they make mistakes along the way, it is normal to make mistakes even if they Nobody likes to waste time hitting the target every time they set a goal, unfortunately things are not like that, everything is a matter of practice to gain experiences and thus grow as people and develop the skills that will help us grow.

We've all heard the old saying that "you learn from your mistakes", but trial and error is really part of how your brain and skills develop.

Now I invite you to think for a moment that you are a baby and that you are learning to walk, to develop that motor skill you have to exercise your legs during several sessions, day and night, day and night, day and night and so on repeatedly until you achieve it. , just as to learn to speak you need to practice several times until you achieve it, although that implies that you will fall on the road if you want to learn to walk because your legs are not used to it and it will be a new experience, when you want to learn to speak you will make a mistake when pronouncing a few words since you need to practice enough to get there.

That will be a process of several months or years, that depends solely and exclusively on you, and no one else, so you have to be persistent regardless of who is around you and wants to make fun of you.

Our mistakes can free us to pursue our goals and learn from them, the former president of the United States in the decade of (1901-1909). Theodore Roosevelt once said, "The only man who doesn't make mistakes is the man who never does anything."

Wow!

Another shocking phrase, they understood well, they interpreted what Theodore Roosevelt meant with that phrase. In theory he said that to learn from our mistakes it helps to have the mental feeling that we can grow or the belief that intelligence is something we can work on and develop. That's what trial and error is all about.

It is enough to believe in ourselves, since, if we start to believe in the words of other people who only see us with the eyes of envy and the negativity of life, destructive criticism will increase because they only judge us by our own appearances without even knowing each other.

If we listen to negative people, there is if the real problem would be.

The problem would be the lack of decision-making, the lack of own criteria. To carry out the activities.

Come on ask yourself something!

If you have all the desire to grow, you would listen to a person who lives his life criticizing others if his life is more miserable than the lives of the people he criticizes. That is, perhaps the old gossip or Mr. Don negativism are part of your achievements, perhaps they are part of your air, For you to pay attention to them.

They are not the ones to come to clip your wings. The fact that they have not been encouraged to undertake does not mean that you cannot.

You know that, if it is frustrating and ridiculous to see professionals work for a minimum salary when they are trained to do better things, and thus they want a country to advance, being conformists, studying a career for 5 years and then end up working something other than what they studied, so they will never grow as people, nor will their country grow.

Then we go back to the same thing, we feel sorry for being entrepreneurs and trying to follow our dreams, but we don't feel sorry for working for a minimum wage. The truth is not funny.

Remember that negative and toxic people are those who only emanate problems, gossip, negativism, therefore it has not guide you to meet your goals. On the contrary, it is only going to influence you so that you end up landing and being one of the bunch.

That only represents the thoughts of envy showing that they suffer from a phobia called the "CRONOS" syndrome. That is, they have a phobia that you overcome yourself because you can displace them. Just like that, think more about yourself, love yourself, love yourself, take care of yourself. As the saying goes.

"No one wants to see a pretty smile on someone else's face."

In this life you are going to meet many people with those characteristics with the phobia that you overcome yourself.

In my experiences to learn from my mistakes, I remember that during my training as an entrepreneur I helped many people to get out of the crisis in my country, I helped many people to achieve their goals by offering them advice, some of them I hosted in my rented room " This is due to the fact that they are close friends and family "and they did not value that friendship that was sincere. At all they do not mind dirtying and trampling that friendship in order to go further than me, trampling me and selling themselves to the highest bidder like Pharisees.

That was wrong, that they made fun of me because they will only approach me with the purpose of taking advantage of something or stealing ideas from a project that they would surely use later for their own benefit. Stealing my ideas. Those are the flies I am referring to and not out of spite, even if it seems.

But for the fact of showing that, even if they try to overshadow you sooner or later you will shine like the eagle that you are soaring to the sky of victory hunting for success from on high.

Those who have not made mistakes will never have experience to comment on the failure of other people, remember that "one learns from their mistakes". This is how our brain and our abilities develop.

Rule Number 10.

Let's relax for a while and think about our future.

Loneliness is not always part of negativity. She can be our greatest ally or advisor in the most difficult moments. It is enough to find inner peace when thinking for a moment about our new life project or rather what will be our next action to reach the heights.

As René Descartes said, also called "Renatus Cartesius", he was a French philosopher, mathematician and physicist born in the 16th century in Sweden, who said "COGITO ERGO SUM". Which in Latin translates "THINK THEN SUCCESS." This will be a good time to think and reflect to put away bad energies. "This is where you end a negative cycle & start with a renewal process.

Chapter 10.

The Solitude Of The Eagle, Learning To Reflect In The Silence.

The loneliness in our lives often presents a great opportunity to find that inner peace that we need, it is that peace whose calm invades our body and our mind.

Let us remember that in this way we can focus on that important life project that always motivates us, but that we leave until tomorrow because the areas of the comfort zone are more important to think about our future for a moment.

That project on which we must focus from now on will be, study ourselves.

Study our environment, the things around us, and the people we hang out with. Many times we take the meaning of the word loneliness the wrong way, because for the common mind you confuse loneliness with spiritual, emotional and even physical emptiness, because it is seen as a frustration.

It is something totally negative for our mind because we tend to think that we have not achieved anything positive with our lives and we do not see progress nor do we have anyone to support ourselves with in these difficult times. Such as a partner, children, friends, siblings.

What do you forget that you have yourself?

Let's look at yourself in a mirror, you will see that you are not only your greatest company, because you are your own teacher and pupil in that moment of tranquility and reflection.

How So, Edbert?

You know, I tell you something my dear friend, Many times we take negative retaliation in this situation, such as crying, screaming, lowering our self-esteem, neglecting our health or feeling ashamed of ourselves.

Why?

If we are alone because we are careless, we are alone because we want to be in tranquility. I said it once and I repeat it again, whoever leans against a good tree gathers good fruit.

Let's take advantage of those moments of solitude to reflect and know what we are doing wrong, in which we must improve to develop and grow as a person, if it is in our plans to create new habits we have to put them into practice so that they are fulfilled. Example we want to improve the figure, we must learn to eat a little more bag as we put it into practice they investigate what is good and what is bad for our diet and above all to know how much we can eat to balance our diet.

We want to see ourselves in good fitness, we must learn to do exercises, we must accustom our body to routines in general, let us remember that we learn from mistakes and that if we do nothing to change our lifestyle for something more direct to the future we will only be doing the same Practice day and night makes the expert, remember that discipline beats talent when it is not trying to maintain itself so do not stop, if you give up today, complain about the future tomorrow

Then don't say they didn't tell you!

If you don't fight to change your future, don't complain about the failures of the present. Despite loneliness you must remember something without pain there is no gain. Do your best, give it all, do your best, don't give up, don't give up. You can't go far with fear. Give your best, give your best no matter how you just find yourself, remember that if you concentrate you can create your own luck and attract those who are necessary to your destination.

The great French philosopher, mathematician and physicist, René Descartes, who is considered the father of analytical geometry and modern philosophy, among his famous phrases said "Cogito Ergo Sum" What he translates into Latin (I THINK, THEN I EXIST ') .

That phrase means a lot to a person who really wants to improve himself, we better think about what we are going to say so that our words do not affect our future, if you excuse me I am going to take this phrase from the great Robert Kiyosaki, who says in his book rich father father Poor that our words serve to leverage us, because it depends on what we say will be how life will go, everything is relative if you are positive you will attract that wealth that is in the soul, I am talking about that wealth that makes us grow as a person , being charismatic and pleasant every time we arrive at a place. Our presence will be unique and our thoughts and values too.

To be stronger is not about developing only muscles, it is also about being more persevering in your battles, that perseverance will help you gain more resistance to achieve greater results and forge a better molding in your body.

Rule Number 11.

If we are going to change something about ourselves, we are going to make sure that it is our way of thinking or acting. Since that will define who we are as a person & what is our life purpose. Only in this way will you plow strong by facing yourself. Facing your fears, making new challenges. If you want the physical changes to be noticed, you have to sacrifice yourself and give your best.

With fear you don't go far, you have to learn to fight for what you want it won't be easy, if you see a person on the street with big muscles and a good body, you will think that in a month I can tone and shape their body, but if you decide Sacrificing yourself to lead a lifestyle similar to that person and practicing in a gym will make you realize that sacrifice and discipline are part of mental and physical growth.

Chapter 11.

Without pain there is no gain.
We must prepare to change.

Despite the doubts and bad times that we may go through when undertaking a project, we have to move on and continue fighting to make that dream come true, that yearned for, that sacrifice for which we are willing to give everything, for everything. , until the expected results are achieved. Or rather give everything for everything to make that dream come true that motivated us to believe in ourselves and be visionary entrepreneurs.

Not everything is rosy!

Let's face it, many times it can happen to us that when we are developing our project halfway, we may be presented with that doubt that creates an uncertainty that will surely leave us an important question that many of us ask ourselves when starting the life project and it is because heck we start in this activity, or rather what led us to carry out this theoretical idea to put it into practice.

You can pass!

It is enough to sit down to reflect and think about our life purpose and because we want to achieve it, who would we be helping when carrying out this activity, as we said before we must learn to take off from the nest and set high goals from small day-to-day purposes, without surrendering, being cowards and throwing in the towel we will not be able to change our future for the better or that of our family that is one of the fundamental pillars to move forward, but how will we be if we surrender so easily.

Doubts can serve to reflect or to make us change that idea for better or for worse depends on the attitude with which you prepare mentally.

Despite the bad times we must move forward and stand up to continue fighting, let's wait, it is not time to give up, we will show the world what we are made of and continue to meet our goals, if it were so easy we would all be successful and not there would be so much difference between people who want to get ahead by going beyond the limits and leave an indelible mark throughout history and people who want to achieve the easy things without doing anything in return, and that is why it is not out of poor, for fearful, for being conformists, it is not enough to think about ideas, you have to patent them, and if you fail it is not synonymous with being bad, that is synonymous with learning through experiences.

If you who are undertaking a business, a life project or an internship to be a professional are afraid of being wrong when you are learning then you are afraid of success.

We must remember something very important No Pain No Gain. Do your best, do your best, don't give up, don't give up. Give your best, give your best a thousand times, imagine that you are a soldier and that you are recruited for a special mission where only you are qualified as the strongest and most experienced person to achieve it, and that if you fail you do not have to to be ashamed if nobody is perfect, in the next mission you will do better because I am sure that sooner or later you will achieve it.

Only then will you get stronger even inside we have that feeling of guilt, or that little doubt where we will ask ourselves how strong I am to resist this battle.

Let's imagine that we are children again.

 And we go on excursions with our family and friends to the beach, and we do not know how to swim, who did not happen to be a child that they took us to the beach as children and it was impressive to see the immense amount of water around us and give them something scary For a moment when we think that we can drown, it is morbid, it is something strange because it scares us, but we are excited to discover if we can not bathe on the beach without drowning.

 Now let's imagine that we are on the beach and we want to learn to swim, we drowned in the first attempt, that fear that runs through our body is an alert signal that will warn our brain that we are in danger and that we must activate the defense mechanisms, that is, fear, that mechanism that prevents us from advancing to our goal and achieving it. Until that sensation of paralysis attacks our body and we say no, no, I don't want to risk it, I am very afraid, something bad could happen to me that is for others that they take risks, I would not go away.

 **Suddenly an older relative arrives, or better said with more experience and tells us calmly, it is normal to feel fear, that is the defense mechanism of your body, the bad thing is to stay with it and do nothing to grow and feed your Fears so that it grows more than you, that is the bad thing, come I will help you nothing bad will happen to you, go let's go swimming.**

At that time we are going to swim for the second time, only this time they teach us so that we can undertake with more courage to give everything for everything. And we practiced all day until we achieved it, although we started with fear, the body would be surprised to achieve it, by not failing this time, by trying and not failing that was a process of change and learning from the experiences acquired, it was not easy but we achieved it so much like this that we no longer want to get out of the water because we think we are fish, that experience will be an anecdote that will stay with us and that we will never forget, since when we leave the beach and return home we will have many stories to tell and anecdotes that will make us reflect so as not to Give up so easily

So much so that the next time we return to the beach we will be able to stare at the sea knowing that it is bigger than us and we can immerse ourselves in it, because already in the past we have gained that confidence in ourselves that allows us to dominate our fears, and there is We will say that it was worth our sacrifice.

My testimony: and that paralyzes you but I had to make a decision and get up from the floor to continue my way all sore, but I still had no choice, my body was still shaking I had to go ahead and test myself again to win that one again confidence that I lost when I got into an accident, that moment I learned from my mistakes, of course I no longer forget how to slow down. You also learn from pain, and believe me a lot.

People who really want to improve themselves and get ahead are those who accept internal changes as one more test to grow and prove to themselves that they are capable of doing to achieve it.

After that, the external changes will be seen, do not forget what we reflect towards ourselves is the energy that the people around us will receive.

Rule Number 12.

 Many times it is good to take shelter for a while to be able to get ahead and renew our repertoire. / renew the set of clothes in the closet, give our best with another aspect, exercise, jog, go to the gym, learn about other cultures, read a good book.

 To then focus on external changes, those that will be noticed from your basic essence, that is, what you reflect as a person. At that moment, not only does your perspective change, but also "your mentality changes & you will begin to see the real changes of look.

Learn to take off from your comfort zone in the best possible way.

Chapter 12.

Eagle Renewal Process,
The Birth Of A (A) Warrior (A).

All this will be a chapter in the book of our lives, people must remember us for our feats not for our fears which we could not sell, it is better to live as a warrior and fight to achieve our dreams to savor glory than to live in poverty. mental and worse still the transitory poverty staying with the tied hands doing nothing.

Once again I ask you what we are afraid of?

We must fulfill our life purpose so everyone will know what we did, they will know our feats!

It is not bad to look good to the world and attract attention with that change in external appearance, but let's face it, physical appearances do not help you to be a better person that will only give you credibility with a few people to sell your image to the highest bidder and that's it. .

Just that, At the end of the day, the day that you do not serve anyone or do not take advantage of you, they will recycle you because beauty ends one day. On the other hand, your brain dies with you because the mind controls the body every time it ages it becomes wiser only if you put into practice the knowledge that you have acquired, that was stronger and more agile.

We are going to define the spirit of an entrepreneur, which is synonymous with innovation, change, the foundation of a new project, and for that you must take risks because an entrepreneur is a person who perceives an opportunity that life offers him and has the motivation fulfilling that opportunity attracts an idea, through drive and the ability to mobilize resources in order to meet this opportunity.

Now if you have confidence in using that idea, you have a good capacity for convocation and conviction, higher than the average because you know how to sell ideas and, above all, you have the ability to obtain results.

It is possible to find many definitions about an entrepreneur, but there are certain common aspects in all of them. And that person has to learn to believe in himself so that this idea becomes a concrete project, a reality that generates some kind of innovation and jobs.

Although not all entrepreneurs are the same, not all have the same abilities to excel.

For them we will mention some basic essential characteristics that every entrepreneur must have:

Positive aspects.

✓   Love to the reader because it is one of the main sources for the acquisition of knowledge and thus you can feed your creativity. Reading is one of the best skills we can acquire.

✓   Energy, to be able to face the difficulties of the beginning and overcome them, without letting yourself be dejected.

✓   Dare to face risks, to embark on adventure.

✓   Conviction in the project itself, as a professional life course.

✓   Decision to dedicate your time, efforts and resources to the project.

✓   Knowing how to enjoy challenges, not letting ourselves be defeated in times of crisis and being able to react.

✓   Accept failure as the path to success.

✓ Having the ability to interact with other people who seek the same development, remember that an entrepreneur works as a team and must know how to create a climate of harmony with his co-workers, his suppliers, his clients, his friends ...

✓ Be a skilled communicator to express your ideas clearly and specifically.

✓ Have technical knowledge about the operational process and marketing. For your project to be successful.

✓ Being creative and innovative, creativity is the main basis for being an agile entrepreneur.

✓ have initiative and responsibility, seek efficiency and quality, be independent, but able to find support among those around them,

✓ be brave, but calculating the risk, be persistent and resistant to failure.

✓   be well informed and do not refuse to go to experts, or face challenges in a positive way.

The entrepreneur must know how to take advantage of the circumstances, and the moment to develop his ideas, although it should not necessarily be his own, but not repeating some mistakes such as:

Negative aspects.

➤   Thinking that all good ideas are novel. The key is not always to create something new and revolutionary, but to solve products or services demanded by the market.

➤   the opposite of the above, believing that everything is invented, entrepreneurs are the ones who drive the world, if there were no entrepreneurial people they would not open the electric light bulb, cars, computers, boats, telephones, medicine, among other inventions innovative.

➤   Believe that the product will sell itself. It is not enough to have a good product, it is necessary to carry out a strategy to publicize the product and sell it.

➢   Believe that by being the first I will achieve success. If the product or service is good, there will soon be competitors willing to outdo it.

These aspects will only lead you to failure for sure, the best way to avoid it is to be positive, read a lot, train yourself and surround yourself with people who know more than you about a better lifestyle, remember that whoever approaches a good tree gathers good fruits .

If you believe in yourself you do not need limits because you break the mold by proposing to leave your comfort zone, this is how battles are won fighting for what you are truly passionate about, fighting to achieve your goals no matter how unattainable you think that will be the goal.

Rule Number 13.

No matter how hard you try, do not give up, life will put obstacles on you, but the limits are set by yourself. Many are the human beings who lose the battle without having fought it before giving up too soon. It is your mind that sets the limits. It is your own self-perception, your own self-image that becomes the barriers that hold back your creativity and limit your self-confidence.

When you feel that this syndrome is about to manifest itself in you, in any circumstance of life, think that you have a formidable "source of neurons" together with the necessary talents so that you can face every situation that life presents you. If you gain confidence in yourself, you will be able to verify it in a crisis, an emergency or a pressing need.

Chapter 13.

Our flight depends on our dreams.

You will never know what you are capable of achieving until you try, remember that life is never going to put you in front of any test that you cannot overcome, the fear of not overcoming it is only in you. The realization of a desire depends on the will that is put into its materialization as well as the will that comes based on the intimate self-belief, that is what will lead you to exceed your limits.

There is nothing impossible everything can be done in this life.

The key is to know how, then it is simple to the most complicated. It's very nice to think that life is fighting against the greatest of enemies. That every day they are going to "attack" us, that everyone has positive thoughts, except you. That enemy is yourself making excuses for not achieving your goals creating excuses, for not giving everything you have within you. Everything so as not to give others that talent that you have.

Everything is good for you, because in reality, you are afraid of being you, of happiness. No matter how much you say what you want, if before you start, you are already integrating into negativism, believing in the limits, in the lies, that others tell you, I assure you that you do not have guaranteed success.

We Become Conformists for Various Reasons:

Due to dependence on other people, low self-esteem, lack of motivation or fear of something, one or more of these factors limit our development and personal growth and prevent us from crossing that barrier that makes you fly high, although not all the people who They surround are flies, and although it sounds offensive. It is a metaphor to name envious, gossipy, ill-intentioned, double-standard people who don't want you to achieve your goals and want to damage your aura through the negativity they possess. These are allusive comparisons to people who like to see others badly and do not contribute anything positive to the growth of others, but on the contrary, you are the one who decides whether to indulge in negativism or not. It is time to leave indelible marks for humanity. I'm talking about those traces that last in the history of our generations.

Those traces that are indelible for humanity, when remembering such a day that your skin crawls when those memories come to your mind to see the glory of success achieved since the feeling of winning with nothing is compared, it is greater than everything Our pride is so great is our faith to believe in ourselves again. To such an extent that we become beings of living light before humanity, in order to see our feats accomplished.

Chapter 14.

Focus on your life project,
Be Visionary The sky is the limit.

Do not prepare to be one of the bunch of people with a simple life, get going. Start now with that life project that you long for, come on, what are you waiting for? It's time to move.

* We are giving our lives for our goals.

You must learn to fight for your dreams and make the achievement of your goals come true, remember that everything is based on a vision, so you must stop looking for cheap excuses and start fighting for that dream that you have longed for so that you can have a personal purpose that motivates you to fight for it and make it happen since it is not enough to just think if we really deserve it or not, then the next step will be to act by starting our creativity.

* Everything begins with an idea and from that idea a vision is born.

Example: Every time we wake up we prepare for the start of a new day, that day for most people only consists of the following:

Waking up for everyday activities whether it's getting out of bed, going to the bathroom, washing up, having a fight, then getting dressed, eating breakfast, and getting ready for places that will keep you 100% occupied for most of the day whether it's work, university, school, sports and recreational activities, among others. The most curious thing is that the same activities are always repeated day, after day, after day, after day, after day, and it is more than what we strive to survive than what we achieve by our own dreams and the more we want to improve our quality more life we have to dedicate to that activity sacrificing the time that we could spend as a family, or in more important things.

Without realizing it, we are struggling to achieve other people's dreams in order to maintain a basic and simple lifestyle. This is where we must worry about fighting to make our dreams come true.

*** You have to learn to control your brain,
Otherwise he will control you.**

Many of us feel bad because when we do a new activity
sometimes things do not go well or as we expect, and that
creates a negative personality in our brain by saving that
memory, and that is the best part of that experience that is
lost. because they don't try again for fear of failure.
Without knowing that experiences are discovered after
failures and that is where learning is born. That is what we
know in my country as "Trial and error.

*** Your opinion is the only one that counts to defend
your project.**

Remember that you are to blame for your own success or
failures. If we start to think that other people are to blame
for our problems and how life is going, that would be a
stupid thing to think that way.

If you are one of those who think this way, then you must
ask yourself something.

Where the hell is the effort, your struggle, your creativity and your entrepreneurial spirit?

It is not a joke, it is reality, where your entrepreneurial spirit and your desire to get ahead!

 The third parties are others, your opinion and your decisions are what will define your future. We cannot go through life blaming other people for our failures.

Take the time that is necessary to realize your dreams, to collect your thoughts and translate your visions into a pencil and paper. We must develop an action plan to achieve our dreams and have a specific goal to achieve it.

* It is time to plan our destiny and to appease our defeat.

Nobody prepares in life to fail, but the reality is that many people fail in life because they do not prepare for success, they just want to be healthy, have a good physical shape and feel better every day but they do not make an effort to change their lives and do not intend to do something to make that happen, they only try to do something that generates peace of mind at a certain time without having to go through so many work processes to achieve something, for example if we intend to lose weight and maintain a A little healthier life we must strive to eat better, not eat so many sweets, sodas, foods with excess fat or that are processed with hormones, among other examples.

All this looks boring, but when you start to fight to achieve your goal you discover something fantastic called "transformation process to reach the desired goal" and that transformation process is called "change" so that change leaves us with a learning process. everything we've had to go through to achieve our goal.

* Prepare for success not for failure, remember that you must put your visions on paper in order to be more clear about your true purpose and how you can achieve it, that is one of the main ideas to start.

* You should also take care of yourself and see who you hang out with, remember that the people you hang out with also influence your mentality, either because of the type of positive or negative information they give you.

* The exchange of ideas with another person must be clear in order to contribute something to the knowledge they provide you.

* Always analyze and organize your thoughts, since your opinion is the most important of all, as well as you must believe in yourself.

* Plan a lifestyle different from the rest of the people around you, do it through your skills and your own criteria.

* Never be left with the doubt of what would happen if you did something, of course if it brings something positive to your life, just do it and that's it.

* Study that project that attracts your attention so much for a certain time to avoid the simplicity of it, that is, study it over and over and over again, each day that passes add something you learn to strengthen your goal to get there to the goal.

* Once you achieve your successes, do not feel satisfied about it, always think about tomorrow and the opportunities that life offers you to achieve new things.

ABOUT THE AUTHOR.

Edbert Josue Rios Toro.I am 27 years old, I was born in Venezuela, in the Miranda State. Coming from the bosom of a humble family. Since I was a child my parents raised me with a discipline and firmness to forge my future since they taught me to fight for it, I have 2 sisters, since I was 8 years old I have practiced Karate Do and Taekwondo. My childhood was fantastic, although I had to learn to work since I was a child to achieve my goals and grow up with that discipline that accompanies me until the sun of today, at the age of 14 I studied computer science and worked on an FM Radio. As an audio operator, Emisora which was my home for professional training for 10 years. There I met many enterprising people with visions to the future because they always bet to believe in themselves, hence I maintain the perspective of being an entrepreneur, in addition to that they became my family. From the production directive, artists, announcers, audio operators, journalists. Because we shared unique moments and ideas to improve as a person. From the most professional to the youngest.

I also studied civil engineering at a public university, I had 2 semesters to finish my degree I had to freeze it, I did not finish it because I emigrated to Peru in 2017.

In mid-October to achieve better opportunities in terms of quality of life, let us remember that my country for years has been going through the worst economic crisis that has been seen in history until now in 2021.

(Venezuela) In 2013. I developed several projects to help various communities to build their homes and repair them by performing ordinary and extraordinary corrective, preventive maintenance. In such a way there was beginning the development of my career. I also brought in civil construction works since I was 16 years old. And he inspected works. My first job was as a painting and finishing contractor.

I emigrated to Peru in 2017. Because, as you know, the crisis has been affecting the country since 2013. Due to political mismanagement. Country where I was accepted by the descendants of the Incas. Peru is a country of entrepreneurs with a great power to exploit, here people are very cultural and bet on development
endogenous, that is, they bet on national production and maintain their roots, that makes them entrepreneurs by the fact of betting on their culture and selling it to tourists, for example, Machupichu, the Inca bath, green coast, long sea as places tourist, / about gastronomy they have infinities of dishes such as: potato a la huancaína, chaufa, lomo saltado, cuy al pisco, humitas, saltado noodle, green noodle, ceviche, grilled chicken, stuffed cause, chili pepper chicken, pachamanca, tacacho with jerky, tacu tacu, among other typical dishes.

Here I learned how to cook some of these dishes since my first job was working in a restaurant as a waiter. Even so, having knowledge in radio, programming and construction. Then I worked in civil construction with two construction foremen who were like my brothers and third parents because they taught me everything they could and encouraged me to get ahead.

11 months later I returned to Peruvian cuisine working again as a waiter and cook to learn as much as I could about Peruvian culture, and to learn to cook. Today I thank the chefs who taught me a bit of their techniques.

At present I am studying the career of Barman and I am taking intermediate English courses. Of course I plan to finish my career in civil engineering because I am one of those who bet on the future and believe in myself because I think that fear does not go far.

Thank you for purchasing this book.

My Wahtsapp: +51 984 741 740.

Mail_ millionaire influences@ gmail.com

Facebook: Influential Entrepreneurs.